At the Recycling Center

By Julia Jaske

I see sorters
at the recycling center.

I see glass at the recycling center.

 I see cans at the recycling center.

I see boxes
at the recycling center.

 6

I see stacks
at the recycling center.

I see plastic
at the recycling center.

I see bottles
at the recycling center.

I see volunteers
at the recycling center.

10 I see bins at the recycling center.

I see jars at the recycling center.

 I see caps at the recycling center.

I see gloves
at the recycling center.

Word List

recycling	boxes	bins
center	stacks	jars
sorters	plastic	caps
glass	bottles	gloves
cans	volunteers	

- I see sorters at the recycling center.
- I see glass at the recycling center.
- I see cans at the recycling center.
- I see boxes at the recycling center.
- I see stacks at the recycling center.
- I see plastic at the recycling center.
- I see bottles at the recycling center.
- I see volunteers at the recycling center.
- I see bins at the recycling center.
- I see jars at the recycling center.
- I see caps at the recycling center.
- I see gloves at the recycling center.

CHERRY BLOSSOM PRESS

Published in the United States of America by Cherry Lake Publishing Group
Ann Arbor, Michigan
www.cherrylakepublishing.com

Book Designer: Keri Riley

Photo Credits: cover: © BAZA Production/Shutterstock; page 1: © Krakenimages.com/
Shutterstock; page 2: © BAZA Production/Shutterstock; page 3: © Juice Flair/Shutterstock; page
4: © SeventyFour/Shutterstock; page 5: © saravutpics/Shutterstock; page 6: © Sakura Image Inc/
Shutterstock; page 7: © Sakura Image Inc/Shutterstock; page 8: © saravutpics/Shutterstock; page
9: © Olena Yakobchuk/Shutterstock; page 10: © RossHelen/Shutterstock; page 11: © Kuznetsov
Dmitriy/Shutterstock; page 12: © Olena Yakobchuk/Shutterstock; page 13: © Pressmaster/
Shutterstock; page 14: © RTimages/Shutterstock

Note from publisher: Websites change regularly, and their future contents are outside of our control.
Supervise children when conducting any recommended online searches for extended learning
opportunities.

Cherry Blossom Press is an imprint of Cherry Lake Publishing Group.

Library of Congress Cataloging-in-Publication Data

Names: Jaske, Julia, author.
Title: At the recycling center / written by Julia Jaske.
Description: Ann Arbor, Michigan : Cherry Blossom Press, 2023. | Series: In
  the community | Audience: Grades K-1 | Summary: "At the Recycling Center
  explores the sights and sounds of the recycling center. It covers people
  and objects found at the recycling center. Uses the Whole Language
  approach to literacy, combining sight words and repetition to build
  recognition and confidence. Simple text makes reading these books easy
  and fun. Bold, colorful photographs that align directly with the text
  help readers with comprehension"– Provided by publisher.
Identifiers: LCCN 2023003179 | ISBN 9781668927236 (paperback) | ISBN
  9781668929759 (ebook) | ISBN 9781668931233 (pdf)
Subjects: LCSH: Readers (Primary) | LCGFT: Readers (Publications).
Classification: LCC PE1119.2 .J368 2023 | DDC 428.6/2–dc23/eng/20230206
LC record available at https://lccn.loc.gov/2023003179

Printed in the United States of America
Corporate Graphics